Life as a Viking

An Interactive History Adventure

by Allison Lassieur

Consultant:
Joel T. Rosenthal, PhD
Distinguished Professor Emeritus
Department of History
Stony Brook University
Stony Brook, New York

D1386094

Raintree is an imprint of Capstone Global Library Limited, a company incorporated in England and Wales having its registered office at 7 Pilgrim Street, London, EC4V 6LB – Registered company number: 6695582

www.raintreepublishers.co.uk
myorders@raintreepublishers.co.uk

ISBN 978 1 474 70679 7
19 18 17 16 15
10 9 8 7 6 5 4 3 2 1

Printed and bound in China

British Library Cataloguing in Publication Data
A full catalogue record for this book is available from the British Library.

Photo Credits

Akg-images, 91; Art Resource, N.Y./The Metropolitan Museum of Art, 17; The Bridgeman Art Library International: Giraudon/Lauros/Trelleborg, Sweden, 75, ©Look and Learn/Private Collection/Pat (Patrick) Nicolle, 35, ©Look and Learn/Private Collection, 72, Photo © Boltin Picture Library/National Museum of Ireland, Dublin, Ireland, 23, Private Collection/Howard Davie, 102, The Stapleton Collection/Private Collection, 46, 101, The Stapleton Collection/Private Collection/Alfred Pearse, 54, The Stapleton Collection/Private Collection/Margaret Dovaston, 30, State Russian Museum, St. Petersburg, Russia/Nikolai Konstantinovich Rerikh (Nicolas Roerich), 85; Capstone: Ross Watton, 36, 42, 65; Corbis: Bettmann, 12; Giovanni Caselli, cover; Mary Evans Picture Library, 79, Douglas McCarthy, 59; Shutterstock: DWPhoto, cover background; York Archaeological Trust, 6

TABLE OF CONTENTS

About your ADVENTURE

YOU are living in Scandinavia during the Middle Ages. Land is scarce, and many men are sailing to other countries to raid their riches. Will you join them?

In this book, you'll explore how the choices people made meant the difference between life and death. The events you'll experience happened to real people.

Chapter one sets the scene. Then you choose which path to read. Follow the directions at the bottom of each page. The choices you make will change your outcome. After you finish one path, go back and read the others for more adventures and facts about life as a Viking.

YOU CHOOSE the path
you take through history.

Most Scandinavian men were farmers at home and Viking warriors in other lands.

Going Viking

The narrow wooden Viking longship heaves and creaks beneath your feet as you sail away from your homeland. You carry only clothing, some food, and your armour and weapons.

The Viking world you know is changing. Your people live throughout the Scandinavian lands of Norway, Denmark, and Sweden. The Vikings in Norway live among rocky mountains and deep, vast waterways called fjords. Vikings in Sweden live in dense forests and experience harsh winters with lots of ice and snow. The lands of the Danish Vikings are flat and rich.

Turn the page.

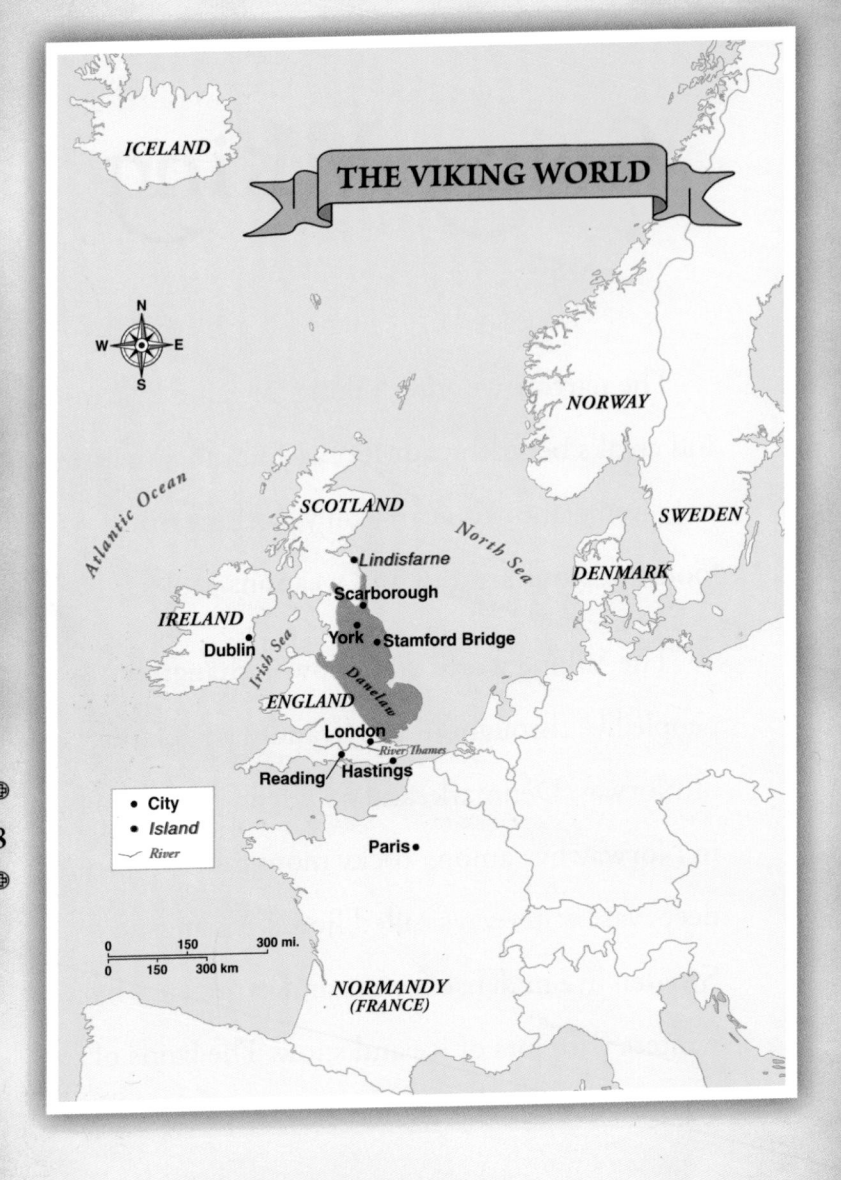

THE VIKING WORLD

ICELAND

NORWAY

SWEDEN

DENMARK

Atlantic Ocean

North Sea

SCOTLAND

• Lindisfarne

Scarborough

IRELAND

York • Stamford Bridge

Irish Sea

Dublin

Danelaw

ENGLAND

London

River Thames

Reading   Hastings

Paris •

● City
● Island
~ River

0   150   300 mi.
0   150   300 km

NORMANDY
(FRANCE)

Everywhere, people try to live by farming the land. But it's not easy. Land is valuable, and landowners are the richest and most powerful Vikings. Now most of the good farmland is taken. There isn't much left for someone like you.

Noble men called jarls are the highest class of Vikings. Freemen are the farmers, soldiers, craftspeople, and merchants. Freemen can own land, but they usually work for wealthy landowners. The slaves are the lowest class in Viking society. Some slaves are Vikings who must work off a debt to their masters. Most of them, though, are captives from other lands.

Turn the page.

There are many ways that a Viking can earn respect. Vikings become good farmers, merchants, and craftsmen. The builders of the elegant longships are the most respected. But that isn't the life for you. You are restless. Something calls you to venture out and see the world.

But you couldn't leave until you learned to be a good warrior. You must be ready to fight your enemies and conquer new lands. You practised with bows, swords, axes, spears, and daggers. The metal mesh shirt you wear, called chain mail, once belonged to your father. It kept him alive in battle. You're sure its luck will also protect you.

And Odin, the father of all the gods, protects warriors during battles and raids.

You look out on the horizon. Is that land you see? What adventures await you?

⊕To experience a Viking raid on a monastery in the year 793, turn to page **13**.

⊕To serve in a Viking invading army in the year 865, turn to page **37**.

⊕To fight in the last battles of the Vikings in the year 1066, turn to page **73**.

Both sails and oars powered the great Viking longships.

CHAPTER 2

Raiding for Fame and Fortune

Foamy waves hiss against the oak sides of the Viking *karvi* ship. The tall sail above you snaps in the strong wind. The carved dragonhead at the prow casts a dark shadow on the water below.

You are crammed into this long, narrow ship with 30 other broad-shouldered Viking warriors. This is your first raid, and an adventure like this is the highlight of a Viking's year. Most Vikings are farmers and craftsmen. But each spring after the crops are planted, they sail away, searching for adventure and riches on faraway shores. They return in time for the harvest. Their ships are laden with gold, slaves, and other treasures.

13

Turn the page.

It is early summer in the year 793. You've sailed for many days in the open ship. Thankfully, the weather is good. You shift uncomfortably on your sea chest. It holds your clothing, bedding, carved drinking horn, armour, and sword.

Suddenly your leader, Gudrik, lets out a wild yell. You see a thin strip of green on the horizon. Land! As you near the shore, you can make out several buildings clustered together. Dark-robed figures run here and there. Gudrik says this land is called Northumbria. The buildings belong to monks and are filled with treasure!

The ship scrapes against the beach, and the men jump out. You excitedly throw open your sea chest and unwrap your sword. Gudrik sees you and says, "Someone needs to stay here to guard the ship."

Another Viking, Sven, notices the look of disappointment on your face and takes pity on you. "He should go," Sven says. "It is his first raid."

⊕*To stay with the ship, turn to page* **16**.

⊕*To go ashore, turn to page* **20**.

"I will stay," you say forlornly.

Gudrik laughs and claps you on the back. "I will return soon and you can have your chance," he says.

He joins the other men running towards the monastery. Shouts ring out as they attack. Soon those sounds are joined by the screams of the monks.

The buildings are too far away to get a clear view, so you climb the prow for a better look. "I hope Gudrik comes back soon," you think. "There won't be any treasure left for me!"

A movement catches your eye. Two people, dressed in robes, are running towards the beach. The taller one is covered with blood. The other one is a small boy clutching a bundle.

Lindisfarne is an island off the northeast coast of England. Its castle was built about 800 years after the Vikings' raid.

"I could capture them as slaves," you think, gripping your sword. "They will fetch a good price at the market."

To go after the boy, turn to page **18**.

To attack the man, turn to page **26**.

The man pulls a sword from his robes just as you grab the boy. You put your sword to the boy's throat. The man drops the sword.

"Get in the ship," you command, but the two don't seem to understand you. Roughly you throw the boy into the ship and push the man in after him. You quickly tie them up. Then you pick up the bundle the boy dropped on the beach.

Inside is a silver chest encrusted with gold and jewels. You open the lid. The chest is filled with coins! You laugh out loud. It's more treasure than you could spend in a year. You return to the ship and begin counting the gold coins as the two prisoners eye you fearfully.

Finally Gudrik returns, carrying a large sack on his back. His eyes widen at the sight of the prisoners and the silver chest full of gold.

"You are the luckiest Viking I know!" he says. "Go now. There is much more left for the taking."

You glance at the shore. A monk carrying a large silver cross is running towards a building. You could easily catch him.

⊕To follow the monk, turn to page **21**.

⊕To stay with the ship, turn to page **27**.

Gudrik also sees the look of disappointment on your face. "Then go," he says. You quickly grab your shield and sword and run towards the buildings.

Shouts fill the air. The area around the buildings is filled with Vikings and monks running here and there. Smoke rises from one of the smaller buildings, and red flames lick at its windows. Three monks dash out of one building. One is carrying a large silver cross. The other two are struggling with a large cloth bundle.

The man with the cross ducks into a large stone building. The other two run around to the back and disappear.

⊕To follow the man with the silver cross, go to page **21**.

⊕To chase the men with the bundle, turn to page **24**.

You run to the large building and take the stone steps two at a time. Your footsteps echo on the stone floor. The man with the cross is trying to escape through a narrow door. You reach him with a few quick steps and cut him down with your sword. The cross clatters to the floor. You pick it up, wipe the blood from it, and shove it into your belt. Looking around, you see two smaller doors leading away from this main area. One of them is open. The other is closed.

⊕ *To choose the open door, turn to page* **22**.

⊕ *To try the closed door, turn to page* **28**.

The door leads into another room. Several wooden tables are near the windows. The tables are covered with parchments, brushes, and small pots encrusted with ink and dried paint. Piles of parchment pages are scattered on the tables. Some pages are blank. Others are covered with writing. Some have been painted with detailed designs and pictures.

You fling the pages and the paint pots to the floor, searching for anything of value. But there isn't anything here. Disgusted, you trample over the fallen pages, covering the beautiful images with mud. On a corner shelf sits a plain wooden box. Inside is a large book. Its cover is made of beaten gold encrusted with jewels.

Bibles were sometimes placed in decorative cases made of gold or silver.

"This is more like it," you think. You rip out the painted pages and throw them onto the dirty floor. You tuck the book cover under your arm and look around. There's a small door at the far end of the room.

To open the new door, turn to page **29**.

To go back the way you came, turn to page **31**.

Racing around the building, you see the two men go through a wooden door into one of the outer buildings. Inside, huge kettles hang in a large fireplace. There are several loaves of crusty bread piled on a table.

Your stomach rumbles at the sight of the fresh bread. It's been days since you had good bread. A clattering noise from the next room tells you that the two men are in there. You draw your sword, and then look again at the bread.

To eat some bread, go to page **25**.
To follow the sound, turn to page **32**.

You tear off a hunk of bread and wolf it down. It's delicious! You shove the rest of the loaf into a pouch hanging from your belt. When you open the door to the room, it's empty. The men must have climbed out through the small window.

A large barrel of flour sits in the corner. There are footprints in the dusty floor near it. As you are about to move closer, you hear a shout from outside. Gudrik is calling everyone back to the ship. It's time to leave.

⊕To leave, turn to page 33.

⊕To stay and investigate, turn to page 34.

You jump out of the ship and run towards the man. At the last minute he pulls a sword from the folds of his robe and slashes your arm above the wrist. You shout in pain. In one movement, you cut his throat. He falls to the ground in a heap. The boy drops his bundle and runs away.

Your wound is bleeding badly. You drop your sword and tear off a piece of the man's robe for a bandage. But the bleeding won't stop. You stumble back to the ship, feeling dizzy and light-headed. Rough hands grab you as you collapse. You think you recognize Gudrik's blonde beard, but everything is going dark. You know that you will never return to your beloved country.

THE END

To follow another path, turn to page 11.
To read the conclusion, turn to page 103.

You shake your head. "This will buy good farmland back home. And two strong slaves will bring even more."

Not long after, the other Vikings begin coming back to the ship. Some lead captured men and boys who will be sold as slaves. Others carry silver cups, gold plates, and jewelled boxes. A few Vikings are wounded, but none are badly hurt. They all board the ship, now crowded with people, and turn towards home.

You're very happy with your first raid. "Next year, I'll return," you think. "And I'll get even more."

THE END

To follow another path, turn to page 11.
To read the conclusion, turn to page 103.

The oak door is heavier than it looks.
You pull hard on the metal ring on the door.
It slowly swings open onto a small room
lined with shelves. The shelves are crowded
with silver cups and plates, gold boxes, and
many other beautiful, expensive objects.
You lift the lid of a large chest on the floor.
Inside, pieces of gold cloth encrusted with
jewels are folded in neat piles. Dropping your
sword, you bend down to grab the cloth.

You're too awestruck by the sight of the
riches to notice a small noise from behind
the door. With one swift movement the door
slams shut, revealing a tall figure behind it.
The axe in his hand hits your chest. You fall to
the floor, dead.

THE END

To follow another path, turn to page 11.
To read the conclusion, turn to page 103.

With one motion you fling open the door. Behind it crouch three small boys, all dressed in dark robes. They are clutching each other in fear. You grin. The boys will make good slaves.

"Get up!" you say. The boys stand, trembling. You look around for something to use to tie them up. As you turn your back, the smallest boy rushes forward and stabs you with a small knife. The blade slides through a gap in your armour and slices the back of your leg.

With a roar, you fling the boy aside. He crashes to the floor. The other two huddle together, crying. As you pull the blade from your leg, blood gushes out. You are horrified at the amount of blood flowing from such a small wound. You can't believe that a child could have hurt you so badly.

Turn the page.

The Viking raiders captured both treasures and people in the raid on Lindisfarne.

As you fall to the floor, your eyes begin to close. Your last hope is that Gudrik will tell your family that you died honourably.

THE END

To follow another path, turn to page 11.
To read the conclusion, turn to page 103.

You leave the building, your arms full of treasure. By this time most of the fighting has stopped. Sven walks past, leading several people tied together with rope. "Slaves for the market!" he says. "I might even keep one or two!"

Several Vikings have brought back people to sell as slaves. Slaves do the hard work on big farms. A powerful jarl might own dozens of slaves.

Other Vikings carry gold and silver objects, pouches of gold coins, and cloth encrusted with gold and jewels. Gudrik is impressed with the book cover you found.

"You have proved yourself in battle," he says as you all climb into the ship. "Next year you will do even better."

THE END

To follow another path, turn to page 11.
To read the conclusion, turn to page 103.

Your empty stomach can wait. When you go into the next room, the two men are trying to hide their bundle in a large barrel of flour.

Before you have time to react, one of the men grabs a large pot from a shelf and flings it at you. You raise your hand against the blow, but the pot hits you square on your head. You're dizzy and your stomach churns as you fall to your knees. The other man rushes towards you with a large carving knife in his hand. You know it's the last thing you will ever see.

THE END

To follow another path, turn to page 11.
To read the conclusion, turn to page 103.

There's nothing here. You leave the kitchen and head towards the ship. By now most of the monks are dead, and the other Vikings have taken everything of value. You're jealous when you see the treasure and the slaves that the others brought back.

Gudrik is sympathetic. "This is your first raid," he says kindly. "Don't worry, you can go raiding with me again next year."

Sven smiles. "You can have one of my slaves," he says, pointing to a small, shaking boy. That's some comfort. As the ship sails towards home, you imagine the treasure you'll find next time.

THE END

To follow another path, turn to page 11.
To read the conclusion, turn to page 103.

You turn over the barrel. A cloud of flour explodes into the air as something large and heavy crashes to the floor. It's a large carved wooden box. Inside are piles of coins, jewellery, and rich embroidered cloths.

Although the box is heavy, you manage to get it outside. Sweat runs off your forehead as you drag it to the ship. Most of the other Vikings are already there. Several slaves sit in the ship, tied together.

Gudrik and the others help you heave the box onto the ship. They stare with amazement at what it holds.

"That is enough to buy a kingdom!" Sven says enviously. "All I managed to get were some silver cups."

Gudrik nods. "You have proven to be a worthy warrior," he says with respect.

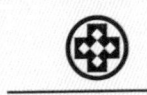

After raids, Vikings loaded up their treasures and quickly sailed away.

As the ship heads out to sea, you're bursting with pride. You imagine the fine farm you will soon have. Life as a Viking is good.

THE END

To follow another path, turn to page 11.
To read the conclusion, turn to page 103.

Viking warriors practised their fighting skills in mock battles.

CHAPTER 3

The great army

"Attack!" shouts the leader of your fighting group. A scream rips from your throat as you dash forward. You raise your axe against the enemy.

Suddenly a trumpet blast fills the air. You drop to the ground, gasping for breath. The "enemies," who are actually other Vikings, laugh. One passes you a skin of water. You gulp from it gratefully. There's nothing like hours of training to make you thirsty.

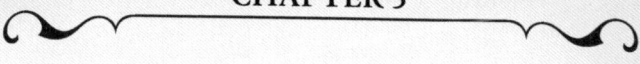

Turn the page.

You hope you won't have to practise much longer. It's now 865. The great Halfdan Ragnarsson and his brothers, Ivar the Boneless and Ubbi, formed this Viking army earlier this year. You and hundreds of other warriors answered their call to conquer the Anglo-Saxon kingdoms of England.

The Anglo-Saxon lands to the south of your homeland are divided into several kingdoms. For several years small groups of Vikings have invaded these lands. You've heard much about the land and wealth those Vikings now have.

The army sailed to England a week ago. Now the huge Viking camp hums with activity. Halfdan calls to the warriors. "Tomorrow we march!" he announces. "This place is known as East Anglia, and its kings are weak. It will be simple to crush them and take the lands for ourselves."

You leave camp at dawn. Halfdan and Ubbi lead the march. Several strong warriors carry Ivar on a shield. The other warriors follow behind. Some ride horses, but you and most of the others are on foot.

"What's wrong with his legs?" asks your friend Eirik, as he points to Ivar.

You shrug. "They don't work properly," you reply. "But he is deadly with a bow and arrow."

Late in the day, your army comes across a large group of Anglo-Saxons. One of them rides over to Halfdan, Ubbi, and Ivar, who watch them warily.

"I am here on behalf of Edmund, king of East Anglia," he says. "We beg for peace from your army."

Turn the page.

"Then give us horses, food, and treasure," Halfdan says. The men ride away. Soon they return with dozens of horses and several wagonloads of food and supplies.

When the Anglo-Saxons leave, Halfdan gives the order to make camp. You are furious. The first chance at a battle, and Halfdan does not take it!

"I think we should attack the nearest village anyway," Eirik says. You agree with him, but think going off on your own would anger your leaders.

⊕To attack the village, go to page 41.
⊕To stay in the camp, turn to page 44.

You decide Eirik is right. "If we wait until nightfall, we won't be seen," you say. Eirik agrees. He talks to a few others who want to go with you. Later that night you all sneak to a small village a short distance away.

Eirik tosses a torch onto the thatched roof of a hut. It instantly explodes in flames. As it burns, several men come running out of the huts, carrying weapons. The screams of women and children mingle with the crackle of the fire.

More houses catch fire. You burst into the houses one by one, searching for anything of value. You rush into one house and gather food, clothing, and blankets. While you're inside, the roof catches on fire. "Time to go," you think.

Turn the page.

Vikings carried axes, daggers, and spears as they charged into battle.

⊕
42
⊕
As you head to the door, you spy a small wooden chest. It's covered with delicate carvings. Surely something of value is inside it.

⊕To leave the house, go to page **43**.

⊕To search the chest, turn to page **62**.

Whatever is in that chest isn't worth your life. You escape the house just as the roof collapses behind you. By now the whole village is engulfed in flames.

You see Eirik running back to the camp. In his arms, he carries a wooden chest similar to the one you left in the hut.

"Look what I found!" he shouts at you. "It has silver dishes and cups inside!"

You wonder if the chest you left was also full of treasure. You shrug, knowing that there will be other chances to get treasure. When you reach the camp, everyone is still sleeping. You sneak quietly to your place by the fire.

⊕*Turn to page* **45**.

"No, we must obey Halfdan," you say.

Eirik shrugs. "I'm going without you, then."

Late in the night you hear the sounds of screaming in the distance. A red light glows against the black sky. Halfdan sees the light and scowls. You wonder if Eirik and the others will be punished for the raid.

To your surprise, Halfdan chuckles to himself. He turns and sees you looking at him. "Good Vikings never pass up an opportunity for raiding," he says with a smile. Now you really wish you had gone with Eirik! Next time you will.

⊕Go to page 45.

The next day the army is again on the move. The horses the English gave you allow you to travel much faster. For many weeks the army travels through East Anglia, but there are no more attacks. Instead, villages offer the army danegeld in the form of silver coins and supplies in return for not attacking.

Finally the army makes a permanent camp near the village of Repton. You and the other soldiers dig defensive ditches and build earth walls called ramparts around the camp. You spend the winter practising fighting and collecting danegeld from nearby villages.

A few months later, the army moves on. It is now 866, and your goal is to capture a town called Eoforwic in the kingdom of Northumbria. In your language, this town's name is Jorvik.

Turn the page.

The army arrives at Jorvik on 1 November, All Saints Day. The townspeople are in church, and the town is lightly guarded. Your army scores an easy victory and settles down to spend the winter in Jorvik.

Townspeople often paid danegeld to the Vikings to prevent raids.

In March 867 Halfdan summons the army. "An Anglo-Saxon force is headed to Jorvik," he says. "We will defeat them!"

A real battle! Halfdan orders part of the army to stand guard in town. He tells the other warriors to go to the Roman walls in the northern parts of the city. The walls once surrounded the entire city, but some are damaged or destroyed.

⊕To go to the Roman walls, turn to page **48**.

⊕To stand guard in town, turn to page **63**.

The damaged Roman walls aren't strong enough to keep out the attackers. When the battle horns sound, you rush forward.

You charge through the throng of fighters, swinging your axe. Enemy soldiers fall at your feet.

Halfdan and several other Vikings are fighting a group of enemies clustered around a tall soldier. As you run towards them, Eirik's voice rises over the noise. "Over here!" he shouts to you.

To help Halfdan, go to page **49**.

To join Eirik, turn to page **64**.

Halfdan notices you and grins, and then goes back to fighting. An Anglo-Saxon falls, and you leap over his body to the tall soldier.

The tall soldier strikes you, and his sword grazes your side. It's only a flesh wound. You surge forward and kill the soldier with one powerful swing of your axe. The man is wearing fine armour and a silk tunic. He must be a king.

Not long after, the battle is won. Halfdan, Ubbi, and Ivar call the Vikings together. Halfdan drags you to the front of the crowd. "This brave Viking killed the enemy King Osberht with one blow of his axe!"

Ubbi lifts your axe high into the air. "Hail, King-Killer!" he shouts.

Turn the page.

That night at the celebration everyone wants to hear the story of how you killed the king. You show off your axe, King-Killer. This lucky axe will be passed down in your family for generations.

In the weeks after the battle, the Viking army settles down again. Halfdan gives you a farm outside the town walls and two slaves to help you work it. You meet a beautiful Anglo-Saxon woman named Acha. You think of settling down permanently, as other Vikings have done.

One afternoon a messenger comes from Jorvik. "Halfdan and Ivar are ready to march again," he says. "They need all warriors to join them."

⊕To march, go to page **51**.

⊕To stay on the farm, turn to page **65**.

After a tearful goodbye from Acha, you join the army as it leaves Jorvik. You promise to return, but in truth, you don't know if you'll ever be back.

It feels good to be on the march again. The Anglo-Saxons flee in terror from your army. Halfdan and Ivar demand danegeld from every village you pass. Some pay. Others don't. You like it when a town refuses, because then you can fight.

Ivar sends for you one afternoon during a break from marching. "I'm putting you in charge of a group of warriors," he says. "There is a wealthy farming village to the west. There is also a larger town to the north, with a church. We must take them. Which would you like to attack?"

⊕To attack the farming village, turn to page **52**.
⊕To attack the town with the church, turn to page **55**.

Supplies are low, so you think the farming village is a good choice. You and a few dozen other warriors mount horses and ride to the village. When you arrive, the townspeople are already gathered in the town square. Several wagons, covered with blankets, stand nearby. An old man steps forward.

"We don't want any trouble," he says.

Something isn't right. The townspeople don't look afraid. They look determined. It is strange that there are so many wagons in the middle of town.

It could be a trap. But it would be suicide for these peasants to attack such a powerful Viking force. Maybe you're imagining things.

To trust your instincts, go to page 53.

To continue with negotiations, turn to page 67.

Glancing at your men, you see that they noticed the same things you did. With a nod, they gallop towards the wagons. The old man yells "They're coming!" The blankets fly off the wagons. Men wearing armour start to jump out, but the Vikings on horseback cut them down. The townspeople scatter, terrified.

"We will teach these English that Vikings cannot be tricked!" you roar. "Take everything of value and burn the village."

The warriors gleefully race through the town, grabbing food, clothing, and valuables. They toss everything into the now-empty wagons. You find several fine horses and a few cows and tie them to the wagons. The screams of the townspeople fill the air. "Serves them right," you think grimly.

Turn the page.

Vikings sometimes set a town on fire after raiding it.

When the townspeople have been either killed or captured, you and the warriors set fire to their houses. You watch the flames, knowing that this will be a message to other villages. Then you turn and head back to camp laden with treasure, supplies, and slaves.

⊕Turn to page 57.

Churches often contain beautiful, expensive treasures. When you arrive, the church is empty. The people must have heard you were coming.

The Vikings scour the church for anything of value. They find little more than a few loaves of bread. "Surely there's more here," Eirik says.

"Check the grounds around the church," you order. "Look for dirt that's been disturbed."

The Vikings search the grounds. The only place where the dirt is freshly dug is in the small graveyard. You have a hunch, so you tell the others to start digging. Soon their shovels hit a wooden chest. It's filled with silver cups and plates. A small pouch holds several rings and jewelled brooches.

Turn the page.

"Ivar will be pleased," you say as you slide a gold ring on your finger. "Each of you take something for yourself. We'll give the rest to the army."

"Can we burn the church?" asks Eirik.

You think for a moment, then say, "No, spare it. The monks will replace their treasures. Then we can steal from them again!"

⊕Go to page 57.

Ivar is impressed with the treasure. "This will support the men for many weeks," he says. "We can trade or sell this for food and supplies."

During the next year, the Viking army travels through England. Most towns give the army food and supplies in exchange for peace. A few try to resist and are destroyed.

In 869 the army returns to Jorvik. Acha is overjoyed to see you, and you ask her to marry you. At the wedding, you tell her that when Halfdan and Ivar call you to battle, you will go.

A year later the call comes. You kiss Acha and your new son, Halfdan, goodbye. For the next year, the Viking army cuts through England. In 871 the army travels to the royal city of Reading. Your army sets up camp near the Thames and Kennet rivers and prepares to attack the city.

Turn the page.

Three days later Halfdan sends out a scouting party. At a place called Englefield, a small group of Anglo-Saxons ambushes the scouting party. Many Vikings are killed. The rest of the party quickly retreats back to the camp.

Halfdan gathers the army and roars, "The only reason any of us are still here is because their army was small. They didn't even have decent weapons or armour! And yet they beat us!"

Your face flushes with shame as Halfdan continues. "The Anglo-Saxons will come again," he fumes. "This camp has two good defences, a large ditch and a palisade along one side. I need strong warriors to defend the ditch. The rest will stay here."

Vikings fought many fierce battles on Anglo-Saxon lands.

To stay in the camp, turn to page **60**.

To defend the ditch, turn to page **68**.

A huge Anglo-Saxon army appears. From the top of the wooden palisade, you watch as the enemy soldiers destroy the smaller Viking force at the ditch. The Viking army leaves the camp and rushes towards the Anglo-Saxons.

The battle is hot and fierce. The two sides are more evenly matched than you thought. King-Killer glints like ice as you cut down soldier after soldier. An arrow hits you in the shoulder, but you pull it out and fight on.

Finally the Anglo-Saxons turn and run. You see Eirik's lifeless body on the ground.

"I will miss you, my friend," you say. "One day I will join you in Odin's hall of Valhalla, and we will drink mead together again."

Over the next few weeks, the Vikings clash with the Anglo-Saxons several times. The Anglo-Saxons win one battle, but the Vikings win the next. In April 871 King Aethelred of Wessex dies at the Battle of Merton. Vikings rule Reading until the next autumn, when Halfdan decides to move the army to London for the winter.

You are tired of battle. When you tell this to Halfdan, he looks thoughtfully at you. "You have become a powerful warrior," he says. "You've earned peace. Ivar has gone to Dublin in Ireland and is now king there. He would be honoured to have you as a personal guard. Or you can return to your farm in Jorvik."

⊕*To go to Dublin, turn to page* **70**.

⊕*To return to your farm, turn to page* **71**.

The thought of treasure makes you forget the heat of the fire. You open the chest. Two silver cups are inside. "These will be worth a fortune at the market!" you think happily. You grab the cups and head for the door. Before you can get out, the roof of the house collapses in flames. You die there on the floor of the burning building, the silver cups beside you.

THE END

To follow another path, turn to page 11.
To read the conclusion, turn to page 103.

You shift impatiently from one foot to the other. Soon you hear the call. The Anglo-Saxon army is near! You and the other men quickly form a strong shield wall.

You laugh when you see the enemy army. It is so small! But as the enemy soldiers attack, you realize that they are stronger than they look. The shield wall breaks apart as the Vikings rush to counterattack. A tall soldier swings his sword at your head. You duck and slice his legs with one blow of your axe. He falls, screaming in pain.

Just then you feel a sharp stab in your back. You gasp for breath as blood flows out of your wound. You die in the streets of Jorvik, never to know how the battle ended.

THE END

To follow another path, turn to page 11.
To read the conclusion, turn to page 103.

Eirik needs your help. He's fighting two Anglo-Saxons.

"So good of you to pick such weak soldiers to fight," you gasp as you swing your axe at the closest enemy.

"You know me," he shouts, swinging his axe at the other soldier. "Always looking for the easy way out!" The man screams as Eirik's axe shatters his shield and cuts into his arm.

You pay attention to Eirik for one second too long. As you raise your axe, the soldier you're fighting slices your legs with his sword. You fall to the ground. With a second blow, he hits your head, killing you instantly.

THE END

To follow another path, turn to page 11.
To read the conclusion, turn to page 103.

You look at King-Killer, which hangs in a place of honour above the hearth. But your hunger for battle is gone. You tell Ivar that you've decided to stay at home.

"I'm disappointed," Ivar says. "You've earned respect as a Viking warrior. But I understand the appeal of a pretty woman and a warm hearth!" He asks you to be one of the officers in charge of Jorvik when the army leaves. You agree.

A good life of farming awaited Vikings who gained fortunes from raids.

Turn the page.

In the spring you marry Acha and plant
fields of barley, wheat, and rye. You and
the other Viking warriors who guard the
town practise fighting. Sometimes you are
called to settle disagreements. Local Anglo-
Saxons make a few attempts to attack Jorvik,
but most of them accept the Viking rulers.
Several Vikings marry local women, just as
you have.

The great Viking army continues to bring
terror to other parts of England. When your son
is born you name him Halfdan. You know that
one day he too will be a great Viking warrior.

THE END

To follow another path, turn to page 11.
To read the conclusion, turn to page 103.

"Pay danegeld and we will leave you in peace," you say. "Whatever is in those wagons over there will do. And you must swear to serve us."

The old man glares at you. "We will give you what is in the wagons, filthy Vikings!"

The blankets fly off the wagons, and men wearing armour jump out. The townspeople pull out weapons hidden under their clothing. The people rush at you, shouting and screaming.

Your horse rears, and you are thrown into the dust. You reach for King-Killer and realize with horror that you dropped the axe when you fell. A farmer stabs you with a pitchfork, and you double over. You know you will die here. You only hope someone tells Acha that you died a brave warrior.

THE END

To follow another path, turn to page 11.
To read the conclusion, turn to page 103.

A large force of Vikings gets into position along the ditch. "I hear that King Aethelred of Wessex and his brother Prince Alfred are leading this army," Eirik says.

Soon the Anglo-Saxon army appears. It's at least twice the size of the Viking army defending the ditch.

Eirik looks at you. "Today is the day we die," he says. You shrug. You know that the gods decided the moment of your death the day you were born. There's nothing you can do about it.

"If I go to Valhalla today, I will kill as many as I can before I leave!" you reply. Valhalla is the hall of the great god Odin. Viking warriors who die in battle go there after death.

With a roar, you and other warriors rush forward. A spear pierces Eirik's chest, and he falls to the ground. Bodies of other dead warriors soon cover him.

A sharp pain goes through your arm, and then another pain pierces your chest. An arrow sticks out of your armour. "Eirik was right," you think as the world goes black. "We will drink mead in Valhalla together tonight, my friend."

THE END

To follow another path, turn to page 11.
To read the conclusion, turn to page 103.

Acha isn't happy about your decision. She tries to persuade you to stay in England. But you've made up your mind. You know that the farming life isn't for you. She sighs, but agrees to go with you. You sell the farm, pack supplies, and ride to the English coast. From there you cross the Irish Sea to the port city of Dublin.

Ivar is glad to see you and immediately makes you one of his guards. Your battle days are over, but you can still serve your leader, and that pleases you. After Ivar's death in 873, you and Acha find that you like Dublin. You decide to make it your permanent home.

THE END

To follow another path, turn to page 11.
To read the conclusion, turn to page 103.

After many days of travel, you see the familiar hills and forests near Jorvik. Acha welcomes you back. You learn that you have a daughter named Mathild, who was born while you were away. You settle into life as a farmer, but you still serve as an officer and a guard in Jorvik. That keeps King-Killer busy on occasion. To your surprise, you're happy with a life of peace.

THE END

To follow another path, turn to page 11.
To read the conclusion, turn to page 103.

Harold Godwinson became king of England in January 1066.

CHAPTER 4

Last glory of the Vikings

You are standing guard in front of the long hall of King Harald Sigurdsson. Harald has travelled the world fighting battles for the last 20 years. You joined him in his recent unsuccessful attempt to conquer Denmark. Now it's 1066, and both of you are back in Norway. You're glad to be home with your beautiful wife, Astrid.

pagenum73

Recently Harald learned that King Edward of England had died. Edward left no direct heir to the throne, so his brother-in-law Harold Godwinson became king. This news didn't please Godwinson's brother Tostig, who wants the throne of England for himself.

Turn the page.

At dusk a man arrives at the long hall. He is dressed well and is riding a fine horse.

"I must see the king," the man says. "I am Tostig Godwinson."

You escort Tostig inside the long hall to Harald. As the two men greet one another, you slip into the shadows to listen. Tostig wants to attack his brother, King Harold Godwinson, and take the throne of England by force.

"I have no great desire to fight a war in England," Harald says.

"There are many powerful men in England who will fight with us," Tostig replies. "We will certainly defeat my brother."

This reconstructed great hall is similar to the houses of wealthy Vikings.

Tostig and Harald talk for several days. Then Harald speaks to you and the other guards. "We will help Tostig defeat King Harold Godwinson," Harald says.

The next few weeks pass quickly in a blur of preparation. You sharpen your sword, which is called Blood-Drinker. It was your father's, and it has served you well in battle.

Turn the page.

In early September Harald's army boards a fleet of warships. You plan to sail with Harald in his magnificent *dreki*, Dragon, with its giant carved dragonhead and red sails. As you head towards the ship, you see a familiar face. It is Grim, another soldier who fought alongside Harald in Denmark.

"I am sailing on that ship," Grim says, pointing to a smaller ship called a *karvi*. "Come with me. We have much to talk about."

⊕To go with Grim, go to page 77.
⊕To stay with the king, turn to page 79.

The days at sea pass quickly as you and Grim entertain the others with tales of your adventures. The talk turns to the battle ahead. "England is full of people," says your friend Bjorn. "It will be hard to attack."

"Bah!" replies an older Viking named Thorson. "If anyone can take the throne by force, it is Harald Sigurdsson."

One day the sky darkens. By nightfall you're caught in a fierce storm. It tosses the heavy ships on the waves like sticks. There is nothing to do but hold on tight and pray to the gods.

A huge wave crashes over the ship. If you don't hang on, you'll go over the side. Grim loses his grip and yells for help.

⊕To hang on, turn to page **78**.

⊕To try to save your friend, turn to page **91**.

It's all you can do to keep your grip as the wave roars over your head. When the wave is gone, so is Grim. Several others were also washed overboard.

Finally the wind begins to die down, and the sea calms. The ship is battered but still able to sail. Once you land in England, you join the rest of the fleet. Tostig is also there with his own small fleet. Your good friend Karl is with him. With Tostig's force, your army numbers about 9,000 men and 300 ships. The huge fleet sails along the coast towards the mouth of the River Humber.

⊕ One morning you spy a village near the cliffs.

⊕ You and several others want to attack it.

⊕*Turn to page **92**.*

"My place is with King Harald," you tell Grim. He smiles and walks to his ship. You board the great *dreki* and find your place among Harald's other men.

Most *drekar* had carved wooden dragons on the warships' prows.

Turn the page.

The trip to England takes several days. One night a fierce storm rages, but only a few ships are lost. Harald's fleet meets Tostig's smaller force on the coast of England. The combined army has about 9,000 men and 300 ships. The massive fleet sails down the coast towards the River Humber.

"See that town, beneath the cliffs?" your friend Karl says. "That's Skardaburg. The English call it Scarborough. There are English warriors there who will attack us."

Another Viking, Bjorn, says, "We must destroy the town." He orders the ship to be run up on the beach. "I need a group to come with me to the cliffs," he continues. "The rest will go into Skardaburg with Karl."

⊕ *To go with Bjorn's group up the cliffs, go to page* **81**.

⊕ *To invade the town with Karl, turn to page* **92**.

Once everyone reaches the top of the cliffs, you begin piling wood and kindling. Soon a blazing bonfire lights up the sky. You find pitchforks and use them to throw burning wood and embers onto the village below. The thatched roofs of the huts catch fire.

As the village burns, its people surrender. You take many supplies from them before sailing up the River Humber.

One morning Harald orders the fleet to stop near a small village called Riccall. "The city of York is 16 kilometres (10 miles) away," Harald says. "It used to be called Jorvik and is one of the most important cities in England. If we can take York, we should be able to capture England."

Turn the page.

You and the other men cut down dozens of stout trees. You use them as rollers to pull the ships up onto the river bank.

You approach Harald as he is putting on his armour. "My king," you say. "The army is about to march to York. What would you have me do?"

Harald thinks for a moment. "I need scouts to ride north to York and report to me," he says. "Or you can stay with me as we march to York."

⊕To stay with Harald, go to page **83**.
⊕To become a scout, turn to page **94**.

"I'll stay here," you reply. You fall in line as the army begins to march. Three kilometres (two miles) from York, several scouts appear.

"The English army is on its way!" the scouts report. You hear the army approaching. The sun glints off their weapons as the English line up near a ditch and along the river. Someone says this place is called Fulford.

"Bring me Land-Ravager!" Harald shouts. Land-Ravager is Harald's personal banner. A Viking named Frirek brings the banner to him. Harald sticks the banner's pole deeply into the ground.

The Viking army races across the marshy ground towards the English army. You must decide where you'll fight.

⊕To attack the swordsmen, turn to page **84**.

⊕To run towards the spearmen, turn to page **95**.

With a huge clash of metal and wood, the battle begins. To your shock, the English soldiers are excellent warriors. This isn't as easy as you thought it would be.

Slowly you and the Viking army push through the English forces. By late afternoon the ditch and the ground are filled with bodies of both English and Viking warriors. You are covered with blood and sweat, but you are still standing.

You're glad to see King Harald is also alive. He is surrounded by so many bodies that you can't see the ground beneath them.

"We have won the battle," Harald says. "I've lost many good men. But the English army has retreated into York. We'll take the town!"

Harald's army triumphantly enters York. The English soldiers flee the town. The remaining townspeople surrender to Harald. You serve as one of his personal guards.

The next few days are busy. As Tostig promised, many English join Harald's army and swear loyalty to him. Harald chooses several officers who will rule over the town and make laws.

Fleets of Viking longships sailed to invade other countries.

Turn the page.

One evening King Harald leaves York and returns to the ships, which are still at Riccall. Most of the Viking army, including you, joins him. Harald is in a merry mood, and he wants to celebrate the Viking victory.

The next morning Harald orders the trumpets to sound. "It is time to return to the castle," he says. "Some of you will go back with me to York. Others must stay to guard the fleet. We'll leave one-third of our men here."

⊕ *To return to the castle, go to page 87.*
⊕ *To stay with the fleet, turn to page 96.*

The morning of 25 September 1066 is sunny and warm. So warm that you wish you could take off your chain mail shirt. The other Vikings feel the same way. There's a lot of grumbling and sweating as the army marches back to York.

Harald and Tostig are riding in front of you. Suddenly they stop. A dust cloud billows into the blue sky ahead of you. Under it, you see the glint of shining shields and bright armour.

"What is that?" Harald asks Tostig.

"It could be an enemy army," Tostig says. "Or it could be English troops who are friendly to me."

Harald frowns. "I don't like this," he says. "We'll stop here until we know more." As the force moves closer, you see it is a large army.

Turn the page.

"Quickly, we must return to the fleet for the weapons and men," Tostig says.

Harald shakes his head. "No. I'll give three horses to our three fastest riders. They will go and get the forces at the fleet."

You know you are the fastest rider in the army. But you also don't want to miss a battle.

⊕To volunteer to return to the fleet, go to page **89**.

⊕To stay with Harald, turn to page **98**.

"I'll go," you tell Harald. He nods. Riccall, where the fleet is beached, is 16 kilometres (10 miles) away. You pray the army can hold off the English until you return.

You reach Riccall 20 minutes later, ahead of the other riders. The Vikings have taken off their armour and are lying on the grass. Eystein Orre, one of Harald's commanders, jumps up when he sees you.

"Get up! The English are attacking!" you shout. "We need reinforcements!"

Quickly the men put on their armour and set off at a run. The heat and the distance slow them down. Their heavy armour and weapons don't help. Some men collapse and are left behind.

Turn the page.

When you get to the battle, the exhausted Vikings can barely fight. The English quickly cut down many of them. Bjorn sees you and shouts, "The king is dead! Harald has fallen!"

You sink to the ground, stunned. King Harald's son Olaf grabs you. "We've got to get back to the ships," he says.

There is nothing left here, so you go with Olaf. When you reach the ships, groups of weary Vikings sit hunched on the ground. As darkness falls, more warriors stumble to the ships. Most are injured, and many die.

90

At dawn King Harold Godwinson of England and his army appear. You are sure he intends to kill you. "Your king is dead and you are defeated," Harold says. "But if you promise peace and friendship to England, I will let you go."

Turn to page **101**.

You jump up in time to grab Grim. But the wave sweeps you both into the cold sea. The last thing you remember is the sound of the howling wind as you slip below the surface of the water.

The Vikings' sailing skills couldn't save some ships from deadly storms.

THE END

To follow another path, turn to page 11.
To read the conclusion, turn to page 103.

With a shout, you and the others rush towards the village. You run into one house and find a sturdy axe and some food. As you step out of the hut, a huge glowing ember crashes onto the ground. You look up to see a rain of fire coming from the clifftop.

"What's going on?" you yell. You leap out of the way of a burning log that is speeding through the air.

"Our men are throwing fire off the cliff!" Karl shouts. "They must not know we're still here!"

Just then a piece of flaming wood hits you in the back. The beautiful tunic Astrid made for you catches fire. You panic and run, but that only makes the fire burn faster.

By the time you fall to the ground, your body is covered in burns. You die a short time later, never to see Astrid or your beloved country again.

THE END

To follow another path, turn to page 11.
To read the conclusion, turn to page 103.

You mount a horse and gallop away. As you get closer to York, you hear a thundering noise. A huge army, spears held high, pours out of the city. Harold Godwinson's army is marching to attack King Harald!

Suddenly your horse rears. You struggle to control him, but it's no use. The English soldiers see you. One draws his bow and lets an arrow fly. It pierces your chest. You die before your body hits the ground.

THE END

To follow another path, turn to page 11.
To read the conclusion, turn to page 103.

You don't think the spearmen will be hard to defeat. But some stand their ground, grimly gripping their spears. You hold up your shield to protect yourself and swing Blood-Drinker at the nearest spearman.

A terrible pain rips into you. You look down to see a spear stuck in your side. You drop your shield and sink to your knees. You die there as the battle rages around you.

THE END

To follow another path, turn to page 11.
To read the conclusion, turn to page 103.

You remain with the fleet. You'll return to York soon and prepare to continue the invasion.

25 September 1066 is a hot day. You and the other Vikings who stayed behind take off your heavy armour and relax in the sunshine.

"Get up, get up!" a voice shouts. A rider is galloping towards you. "The English are attacking!" he says. "We need reinforcements!"

Quickly you pull on your chain mail shirt and helmet. You set off at a run with the other warriors. It's 16 kilometres (10 miles) to York, and soon you become tired. But you must push forward. The king needs you.

You keep running, but your legs are moving more and more slowly. Finally you collapse at the side of the road. You try to peel off your armour, but your fingers don't work right. Sinking against a tree, you watch everyone disappear.

Maybe if you rest for a bit, you'll be all right. Your eyes slowly close. You die there of heat exhaustion, never knowing what becomes of the invasion of England.

THE END

To follow another path, turn to page 11.
To read the conclusion, turn to page 103.

Harald orders the men to form a long line, shield to shield, across the field near Stamford Bridge. You stay with Harald's personal guards in the front of the army.

Twenty English riders in full armour ride to Harald and Tostig. One of the horsemen calls out, "Is Earl Tostig in this army?"

Tostig rides forward. "I cannot deny that you will find him here."

"Your brother, King Harold of England, says that if you don't fight against him, you can rule one-third of his kingdom."

"If I accept his offer, what will you give my friend King Harald Sigurdsson for his trouble?"

The rider smiles. "As much English ground as it takes for his grave."

That is a terrible insult. You reach for your sword. Harald puts his hand on your shoulder and whispers, "Save your strength for battle." You drop your hand to your side.

"Then tell Harold to get ready for war!" Tostig bellows, drawing his sword. The rider gallops away.

Harald asks Tostig, "Who was that man?"

"That was my brother, King Harold Godwinson," Tostig replies.

"Had I known it was the king," Harald says angrily, "I would not have let him go."

"I purposely didn't tell you who he was," Tostig says. "I would be his murderer if I betrayed him." You understand Tostig, but you still would have liked to kill the English king.

Turn the page.

With a blast of trumpets, the Viking army attacks. An arrow whizzes through the air and strikes Harald in the neck. He falls to the ground, and you know he's dead. You swing Blood-Drinker wildly, killing an enemy soldier before an arrow thuds into your chest.

"At least I will die with honour," you think as you fall beside your king.

THE END

To follow another path, turn to page 11.
To read the conclusion, turn to page 103.

The English army defeated the Vikings at Stamford Bridge.

You all swear the oath. The king seems satisfied and leaves. You all climb into a few ships. Of the thousands of Vikings who sailed with Harald, only a few hundred survive. As the ships sail away, you wonder what will become of Norway and the Vikings.

THE END

To follow another path, turn to page 11.
To read the conclusion, turn to page 103.

Viking Canute the *Great* (centre) ruled England from 1016 to 1035.

CHAPTER 5

The end of Viking power

The Viking raids in England began with the monastery at Lindisfarne in 793 and continued for more than 50 years. The lightning-fast Viking ships sailed up rivers, attacked quickly, and disappeared before anyone could sound an alarm.

In 850 everything changed when the first Viking Great Army landed in England and stayed over the winter. Each year Viking armies landed in England and France. The Great Army of 865, led by brothers Ubbi, Halfdan, and Ivar Ragnarsson, was one of the most effective.

The Great Army caused much destruction in England. But its members also established the city of Jorvik, now called York. The army split up around 870. Halfdan took part of the Viking army and another Viking, Guthrum, led the rest.

By 876 Halfdan and Guthrum had conquered all of England except Wessex. This kingdom was ruled by Alfred the Great. Halfdan became the first Viking ruler of Northumbria. He was killed in a sea battle near Ireland in 877.

In 886 Guthrum made peace with Alfred the Great. The peace treaty gave the Vikings almost half of England. This area in northern and eastern England was later called the Danelaw.

Vikings also explored other lands. In 1000 Leif Eriksson landed in North America, most likely in what is now Canada. He was the first European to see the New World.

Although Eriksson's North American settlement wasn't successful, Vikings lived in Iceland and Greenland for many years. The last Viking settlements in Greenland died out in the 1500s, probably because of changes in climate.

The Battle of Stamford Bridge in September 1066 is considered the last great Viking battle. Viking King Harald Sigurdsson and his English ally, Tostig Godwinson, were killed during this Viking defeat. About three weeks later, Duke William II of Normandy defeated English King Harold Godwinson at the Battle of Hastings.

Almost 1,000 years have passed since the age of the Vikings, but these warriors are remembered for their strength and bravery in battle. The Viking ideal of honour and loyalty to the leader and the family still rings true today.

TIME LINE

793 – The Vikings raid the monastery at Lindisfarne, England, beginning the Viking Age in Europe.

795 – Vikings raid the monastery at Iona, Scotland.

830–850 – Viking raiders attack England and the French coast.

841 – Vikings capture the town of Dublin, Ireland.

850–851 – For the first time, Vikings remain in England after raiding.

865 – The Great Army of Vikings, led by Halfdan and Ubbi Ragnarsson and Ivar the Boneless, lands in East Anglia.

866 – The Great Army invades the city of Eoforwic, which they call Jorvik.

870 – The first Vikings reach Iceland.

871 – The Vikings battle the Anglo-Saxons, led by King Aethelred and his brother Alfred; Aethelred is killed in battle and Alfred becomes king.

877 – Halfdan Ragnarsson is killed in a sea battle near Ireland.

886 – Alfred the Great and Guthrum sign a peace treaty, which gives Vikings control of half of England.

902 – Irish kings force the Vikings out of Dublin.

919 – Vikings return to power in Dublin.

986 – Erik the Red establishes a settlement in Greenland.

1000 – Leif Eriksson, son of Erik the Red, lands in North America.

1014 – Irish King Brian Boru defeats the Vikings at the Battle of Clontarf.

1016–1035 – Viking King Canute the Great rules England.

1042 – Edward the Confessor becomes king of England.

1047 – Harald Sigurdsson becomes king of Norway. He is known as Hardrada, which means "hard ruler."

1066 – Edward the Confessor dies and Harold Godwinson becomes king of England.

25 September – Harold Godwinson defeats Harald Sigurdsson at the Battle of Stamford Bridge.

14 October – Duke William II of Normandy defeats Harold Godwinson at the Battle of Hastings.

OTHER PATHS TO EXPLORE

In this book you've seen how the events surrounding Viking warriors look different from three points of view.

Perspectives on history are as varied as the people who lived it. You can explore other paths on your own to learn more about the Vikings. Seeing history from many points of view is an important part of understanding it.

Here are some ideas for other Viking points of view to explore:

+ Although most Viking warriors were men, some women also fought bravely. What were their lives like?

+ The Vikings destroyed many towns during their raids. What would it have been like to experience a Viking raid of your town?

+ Many Vikings left Scandinavia and set out for distant lands. Greenland was uninhabited and nearly unknown when they settled there. What was it like for Vikings trying to start a new life in a strange land?

READ MORE

All About Viking Beliefs, Tristan Boyer Binns (Raintree, 2014)

Vicious Vikings, Terry Deary (Scholastic, 2013)

Viking (Eyewitness) (Dorling Kindersley, 2011)

Viking World, Philippa Wingate (Usborne, 2013)

INTERNET SITES

Visit these sites for more information about the Vikings:

www.bbc.co.uk/schools/primaryhistory/vikings/

www.ngkids.co.uk/did-you-know/10_facts_about_the_vikings

www.nms.ac.uk/explore/play/discover-the-vikings/

GLOSSARY

chain mail – armour made of metal links

danegeld – treasure and silver coins paid to Vikings to keep them from attacking

dreki – largest of the Viking longships; the prow and stern were carved to look like the body of a dragon

jarl – Viking nobleman

mead – alcoholic drink made from honey

monastery – group of buildings where religious men called monks live and work

karvi – type of longship with 12 to 32 oars; some karvi had prows carved to look like dragons

palisade – tall fence used for defence

rampart – surrounding wall of a fort built to protect against attack

Valhalla – the god Odin's hall where Vikings who die in battle go

BIBLIOGRAPHY

Brent, Peter. *The Viking Saga.* New York: Putnam, 1975.

Chartrand, René. *The Vikings: Voyagers of Discovery and Plunder.* Oxford, U.K.: Osprey, 2008.

Hall, Richard. *The World of the Vikings.* New York: Thames and Hudson, 2007.

Keynes, Simon, and Michael Lapidge, translators. *Alfred the Great: Asser's Life of King Alfred and Other Contemporary Sources.* New York: Penguin, 1983.

Logan, F. Donald. *The Vikings in History.* New York: Routledge, 2005.

Magnússon, Magnús. *Vikings!* New York: E. P. Dutton, 1980.

Marren, Peter. *1066: The Battles of York, Stamford Bridge, and Hastings.* Barnsley, U.K.: Leo Cooper, 2004.

Pörtner, Rudolf. *The Vikings: Rise and Fall of the Norse Sea Kings.* New York: St. Martin's Press, 1975.

Sawyer, P. H. *Kings and Vikings: Scandinavia and Europe, AD 700–1100.* New York: Methuen, 1982.

Walker, Ian W. *Harold: The Last Anglo-Saxon King.* Thrupp, Gloucestershire, U.K.: Sutton, 1997.

INDEX